Managing Editor
Karen J. Goldfluss, M.S. Ed.

Editor-in-Chief
Sharon Coan, M.S. Ed.

Illustrators
Howard Chaney
Bruce Hedges

Cover Artist
Lesley Palmer

Art Coordinator
Kevin Barnes

Art Director
CJae Froshay

Imaging
James Edward Grace

Product Manager
Phil Garcia

Publisher
Mary D. Smith, M.S. Ed.

D1122191

Stars & Planets

SUPER SCIENCE ACTIVITIES

Written by Ruth M. Young, M.S. Ed.

Teacher Created Resources, Inc.
6421 Industy Way
Westminster, CA 92683
wwwteachercreated.com

ISBN: 978-0-7439-3663-7

©2002 Teacher Created Resources, Inc.
Reprinted, 2009
Made in the U. S. A.

Table of Contents

Introduction

Astronomy is perhaps one of the oldest sciences, since it was originated by the earliest civilizations. They used the stars to predict when to plant and harvest their crops and invented calendars and time according to the annual and daily motions of the sun. They invented star patterns (*constellations*) to create star maps of the sky. These ancient astronomers (*astrologers*) were interested in recording and then predicting the motions of the wandering stars (*planets*) and the moon, which they believed controlled human destinies. Modern astronomers recognize the contributions of these early scientists. Although we no longer believe in astrology, the legacy of observations made by the astrologers provided the foundation for mankind to learn about what we see in space and ultimately to venture out for a closer look.

This book is designed to help students see how easy it is to learn by observing what is happening in the sky, both day and night. It begins with a simple experiment to show students how they can use their shadows to learn about the sun's daily motion. They discover that the sun appears to move east to west, making their shadows change length and direction during the day. Proving that it is Earth which is doing the moving, and not the sun, was difficult for our ancient ancestors. For over 2,000 years they believed that Earth was the center of all we see in space, and everything—including the sun, moon, planets, and stars—revolved around our planet. Many of our young students have these same misconceptions. By following the shadow activity with a demonstration using a globe with a paper figure on it and the sun, the children can see that the shadow's changes can be created by a rotating Earth.

The mystery of why the moon changes its shape is solved through nightly observations and drawings students make of the moon from first crescent to full phase. This data is collected each night and then brought to school to be recorded on a classroom chart. The data is applied during an activity to simulate the phases of the moon, using Styrofoam balls as the moon and a bright light as the sun. Even young children can begin to solve the mystery of the cause for the phases of the moon through these activities.

Using the ancient constellations, students begin to find their way around the night sky. They look at the pictures ancient astronomers superimposed on the star patterns and then invent their own modern constellations from these same patterns. Using the dot-to-dot method, the children find the dipper and the bear hidden in the sky. They place this pattern over the outline of a bear which Native Americans invented long ago for this set of stars. The students hear the story which explains how *Ursa Major* and *Ursa Minor* (*Big Bear* and *Little Bear*) got their long tails.

Students also learn about the comparative sizes of the planets and their distances from the sun and each other. This is done using scale models created by the teacher to enable students to experience these concepts concretely. Finally students explore comets and simulate the ingredients that make up comets.

The students' families are involved throughout these activities which take place during and after school. Thus, the child has the opportunity to show his or her family that science is really fun.

Me and My Shadow

Teacher Information

The sun appears to move east to west across the sky each day. Most young children believe this is caused by the sun's motion. This lesson is designed to help children correct this misconception. A quick assessment of their understanding of the concept is done prior to the lesson. Using their own shadows and the shadow of a paper child on a globe, students learn through a simulation how the sun's apparent motion can be caused by Earth's motion.

Overview: *Students will use shadows to demonstrate that Earth is moving, not the sun.*

Materials

- chalk
- large globe
- file card
- adhesive putty
- scissors

Pre-assessment

- Distribute paper to the students and have them make drawings that describe how they think day and night occur.
- Tell them to label their drawings. Let them share these in small groups.
- Save these drawings to compare them with the post-assessment drawings.

Activity One

1. Early on a sunny day, take the students to an area where paving is available to do this activity. Have the students spread out so they can all see their own shadows. Explain that you will give them some time to play with their shadows to see what they can learn about them. Demonstrate how this can be done safely by pointing out your own shadow and how you can change its shape. Don't give too many suggestions; you want the students to discover on their own. Let students have about five minutes to investigate their shadows and then have them share what they have learned. Be sure they have discovered that their shadow looks just like their shape but shows neither color nor complete features, such as a face.

2. Divide the students into groups of three and provide a piece of chalk for two members of each group. Explain that one member of the group will create a shadow and hold the pose while the other two draw around the shadow. They should begin by drawing around the shoes so the person will know exactly where he or she is standing. The entire shadow should be outlined. Let the student whose shadow has been drawn compare it to his or her actual size by lying on it with his or her heels in the outline of the feet. (*Alternate method:* Use string which is the same height as the student to compare the length of the shadow and the student.) Tell the students they will return to this same location in a few hours to see what has happened to their shadows.

Activity One *(cont.)*

3. Return to the shadow site about noon and have each student stand on the outline of his or her shoes. Let the students discover what has happened to the shadow. (*It will have moved from west to east.*) Remeasure the length of the shadow in the same way as before. Ask the students what they observed. (*The shadow will be smaller than before.*) Have the same person pose for another shadow outline, standing in the original shoe outline in the same pose.

4. Return to the shadow just before school ends. Let the students study the shadows and measure them again. Discuss what has happened throughout the day. (*All shadows changed size from large to small to large again. They all moved from west to east during the day.*) Tell the students to think about what they observed today and to return tomorrow with ideas of why this happened.

Activity Two

1. Do this the day after activity one so the shadow outlines will still be visible. Cut a one-inch (2.5 cm) high figure of a child from a file card and use adhesive putty to hold it on the globe in the location of the school. Take the globe and students to their shadow outlines at the same time in the morning as was done the previous day. Ask the students to stand in their outlines again. Let students discuss what they see. (*The shadows should be close to the outlines made on the previous day.*)

2. Set the globe in the sun and turn it so the shadow of the paper child is visible and lines up with the shadows on the ground. Tell students to pretend they are the paper child standing on the globe. Have them watch as you turn the globe west to east in a counterclockwise direction. (*The shadow will move and become shorter.*) Stop the globe when the shadow is shortest. Ask the students what caused the shadow to change. (*direction of the sun as the globe [Earth] moved*) Help them to understand that to the child on Earth, the sun appeared to climb higher in the sky, moving east to west. Continue to turn the globe to show that the shadow becomes long again and disappears as the child moves into night.

Closure

Repeat this so students will once again be able to observe the shadow change. Ask them to explain what the sun would look like to the child on Earth at various locations. Have students discuss this and let them turn the globe themselves to develop a better understanding of this abstract concept. (*Note:* Many young children have the misconception that we live beneath "the skin" of the globe. This may be because they see blue sky overhead and oceans are blue. Be sure to point out that we live on the surface of Earth and that the sky is not shown on the globe. A photograph of Earth as seen from the space shuttle or the Apollo mission would help to reinforce this concept.)

Assessment

Return to the classroom and have students make another labeled drawing to explain how day and night occur. Compare this with their pre-assessment.

Making a Sundial

Overview: *Students will make a sundial.*

Materials

- copies of the sundial and protractor (page 7)
- compass for locating north
- transparency of sundial and protractor
- string (5 inches/13 cm per student)
- chalk
- card stock
- rulers
- clear tape
- scissors

Teacher Background

Sundials were among the first clocks, the date of their origin is unknown. There are horizontal and vertical ones can be found all over the world. The angles on the sundial and the angled shadow maker (*gnomon*) which shows the time, vary with the latitude. The sundial in this lesson is set for a 40° latitude. If you are not at this latitude, there were be a slight change in the time as shown on the dial. Sundials only show local time, which is different than the standard time for your time zone (the time shown on your clock). Also, during daylight savings time you will need to add an hour.

Lesson Preparation

- Copy the sundial on to card stock to make enough for each student.
- Copy the protractors on regular paper to distribute to each student.

(Hint: Duplicate the images to fit more than one on a page before copying them.)

Activity

1. Distribute a copy of a sundial, string, scissors, and a copy of a protractor to each student. Have them cut out the sundial and protractor. Show the transparency of the sundial and sundial. Use the protractor to show that the angles on the sundial are not equal to each other. Also point out that the noon line points north and that the times are divided between on either side of this line. Ask the students why only the hours of 7 A.M.–5 P.M. are shown. (The sundial only works when the sun is out. Some sundials will show 5 A.M.–7 P.M.)

2. Explain to the students how to fold their sundial and then, cut the slits in it. Show them how to attach the string through the slit at the bottom and secure it with clear tape. Demonstrate how to pull this sting to the top slit and, after inserting it, measure the angle made at the bottom. Once this angle shows 40°, fasten it with clear tape. This may require making the slit a bit deeper.

3. Let the students take their sundial outside, along with a piece of chalk. Use the compass to determine north. (Note: This will be magnetic north; actual north is slightly west or east of this, depending upon where you are located. The difference will not be very noticeable since the sundial is only an approximation of the correct time.)

4. Have the students move their sundials so the strings all point north. They should read the time from their sundial and compare it with the actual time. Have them draw around the base of the sundial with chalk.

Closure

Let the students take their sundials out at half hour intervals for a few times to check the time.

Making a Sundial *(cont.)*

Sundial and Protractor

Directions

1. Cut a slit along the dashed line. Attach a string by sliding it through the slit toward the west-east line. Create a 40 degree angle (as shown) with the base of the sundial. Secure the end of the string to the back of the sundial with tape.

2. Lay the sundial on level ground in the sunlight. Point the string north. Read the time marked by the shadow of the string across the face of the sundial. It should be close to the actual time, but may be one hour off if daylight savings time is in effect. Draw around the base of the sundial with chalk. Take it up and return an hour later to once again check the time on the sundial.

NORTH

Fold the sundial in half along this line to form a 90° angle.

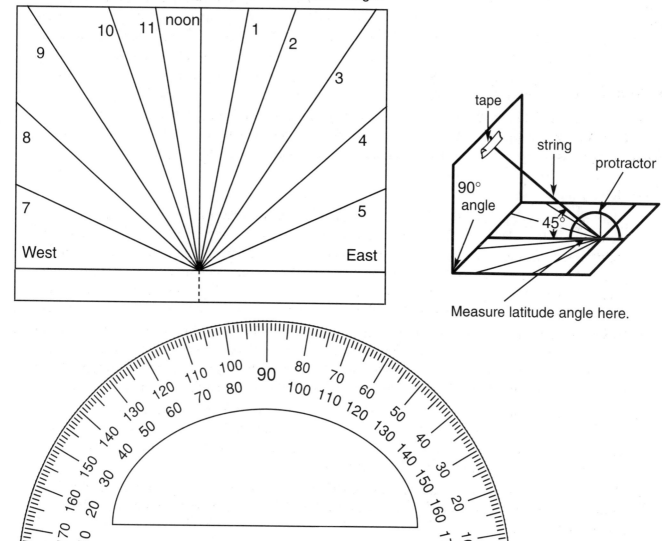

What Shape Is the Moon Tonight?

Overview: *Students will gather data about the phases of the moon.*

Materials

- copies of Student Moon Record sheet (page 10)
- parent letter (page 9)
- Classroom Moon Record (page 11)
- glue

- small bulletin board covered with black butcher paper
- 16–3/4 inch (2 cm) white, self-adhesive dots
- white and orange crayons
- pencil

Lesson Preparation

Make a transparency of the Classroom Moon Record and project it onto the black paper. The diameter should stretch at least two feet (60 cm). Use white crayon to trace the arc and pencil to make the small marks. These represent the positions of the moon during half the month.

Pre-activity (Begin this lesson two days after the new moon. Check the weather section of the newspaper or a calendar for this date.)

1. Distribute the parent letter and Student Moon Record. Discuss these with the students so they understand how to record the phases of the moon every evening at the same time.
2. Show them the Classroom Moon Record and say that each day you will place a moon shape there showing what they report in the evening sky. Point out where the sun is shown on the record.
3. As students report the moon shape each day, cut an adhesive dot into that shape and place it on the chart. The first one will be on the first or second mark, depending upon how many days past the new phase this record is begun.
4. After three days of recording data, have students predict how the next day's phase will look. Draw all predictions on the board and check them the next day. If a night is cloudy, have students predict what the shape of the moon was, based on the phases before and after.

Closure

- Review the positions and phases of the moon relative to the sun's position. Repeat the activity with the balls and light so students can see how this represents what they are recording.
- About two days after the moon is full, look for it in the morning sky in the west. Its phase will change to gibbous, quarter, and then a crescent as it gets closer to the sun each day. Be sure they see that it is now the left side of the moon which is illuminated by the sun.

Extender

Make a daytime record of moon phases after the full moon. Project the moon record on blue paper and make the same markings. Since this is a day view, the sun should appear in the east (sunrise). Even though students will view the moon after the sun has risen, the sun can be in the east. The full moon would be in the west as the sun is rising. As the moon changes to gibbous, circles can be cut according to views seen and glued along the arc, continuing west to east, as the moon moves around Earth. The last quarter phase would be 90° between the east and west; the final crescent would be very close to the sun as it rises in the east.

What Shape Is the Moon Tonight? *(cont.)*

Parent Letter for Moon Observations

To the Teacher: The time for sunset can be found in most weather reports on TV or in the newspaper. Add the time to the letter which is 30 minutes after sunset, the time students should observe and draw the moon.

Date_____

Dear Parents,

We are studying the changing shapes of the moon (phases), and each child has been asked to look at the moon and draw it each evening. (A helpful chart of the moon's phases appears below.) Please help your child with this activity. It is important that he or she observe the moon at about the same time each evening. We will be viewing the moon approximately 30 minutes after sunset which will be about_____p.m. Have your child go outside to get a good view of the moon. Ask him or her to draw exactly what is seen and bring the drawing to school the next day. We will be using those drawings to place the correct phase on a Classroom Moon Record daily.

It will take approximately two weeks for us to gather the data we need for this study. This activity will help your child understand that the moon is constantly changing its shape as well as its position every day.

Thank you for helping your child learn about the moon. You are always welcome to come visit our class to see our moon record.

Cordially,

_____

Phases of the Moon

New Moon	Crescent Moon	First Quarter Moon	Gibbous Moon

Full Moon	Gibbous	Last Quarter	Last Crescent

What Shape Is the Moon Tonight? *(cont.)*

Student Moon Record

Name:_____ Date: _____

Go outside where you can see the moon clearly. Make a drawing of the moon each evening about_____P.M. Write the date and time. Bring this record to school each day.

Date: _____ Time:_____	Date: _____ Time:_____	Date: _____ Time:_____
Date: _____ Time:_____	Date: _____ Time:_____	Date: _____ Time:_____
Date: _____ Time:_____	Date: _____ Time:_____	Date: _____ Time:_____
Date: _____ Time:_____	Date: _____ Time:_____	Date: _____ Time:_____
Date: _____ Time:_____	Date: _____ Time:_____	Date: _____ Time:_____

What Shape Is the Moon Tonight? *(cont.)*

Classroom Moon Record

To the Teacher: Make a transparency of this page and project it onto a large piece of black butcher paper. The horizon line should be at least two feet (60 cm) long. Use white crayon to trace the arc and horizon. Trace the marks along the arc in pencil so they are not seen. These are the positions of the moon phases. The phases begin with the new moon at the western horizon, first quarter moon 90 degrees from east and west, and full moon on the eastern horizon.

Color one of the self-adhesive dots orange to represent the sun. Place it on the classroom chart in the location indicated on this drawing, to represent the sun's position 30 minutes after sunset.

The sky is represented by the arc. The view is to the south.

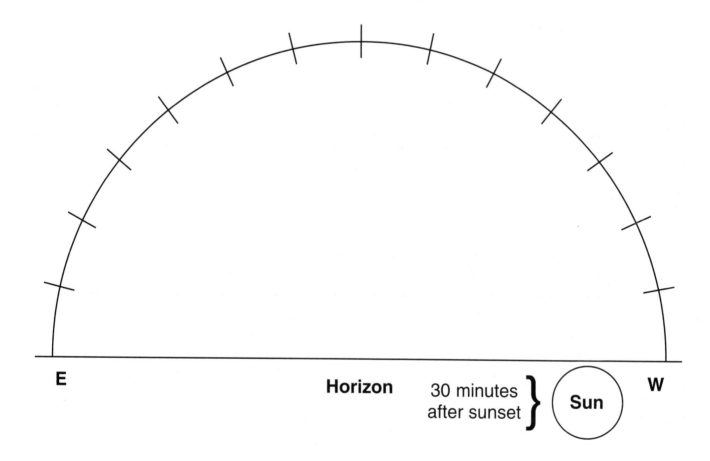

Moon Shapes

Overview: *Students will discover what causes the phases of the moon.*

Materials

- transparency of Moon Phase Cutouts (page 14)
- clamp-on light fixture with 150 watt bulb (*optional:* overhead projector)
- three-inch (8 cm) Styrofoam balls (one per student)
- sticks (one per ball)
- white glue (*optional:* hot glue)
- transparency of The Phases of the Moon (page 15)
- large ball (e.g., soccer)
- sticky notes

Lesson Preparation

- Push a stick halfway into each Styrofoam ball, withdraw it, and pour liquid glue into the hole. Reinsert the stick and let it dry.
- Clamp the light onto the wall in the front of the room, at least six feet off the floor. Clear an area in front of the light for all students to be able to gather near but with room to spread out.
- Place a sticky note on the large ball, large enough to be clearly seen from six feet away.

Activity

1. Ask students if they have noticed the shape of the moon lately. Let them draw on the board the shapes they have seen the moon take.

2. Put the moon phase cutouts on the overhead (or board) and have the students suggest how they should be arranged in the order they are viewed. (Do not expect accuracy just yet.)

3. Ask them if they can explain why the moon changes shape.

4. Explain that they are going to do an activity which will show how the moon changes its shape. Distribute a ball on a stick to each student. Gather near the light and darken the room (the darker the better). Arrange the students so that no one is standing in another child's shadow.

5. Tell the students to watch you as you demonstrate how they are to move. Explain that the ball is the moon and their head is Earth. They are standing on Earth looking at the moon. Hold the moon (ball) so it covers up the light and have the students do the same. They should notice that they cannot see any light on the moon; this is the *new* phase.

6. Slowly turn to your left (students should follow) and have them look for the thin crescent of light on the right side of the moon. Let them know that about two days have passed since the moon was new, and it is now in the *crescent* phase.

7. Continue to turn slowly to the left, stopping to show the phases of *first quarter, gibbous, full, gibbous, last quarter, last crescent,* and back to *new*. Tell the students this whole trip of the moon around Earth takes about 29 days or one month.

8. Have the students continue to revolve slowly, holding their moons slightly above their heads and seeing the different phases as you call out the phase names. Move among the students to be sure they are seeing the correct shapes. Let them do this several times.

Moon Shapes (cont.)

Closure

- Ask the students to rearrange the moon phases on the overhead (or board) to show what they have learned about the order of the phases. Let them go through the motions again of creating the moon phases with the Styrofoam balls.

- Turn on the lights and have the students sit in a large circle. Use the large ball to represent the moon and let the students represent Earth. Tell the students that we see only one side of the moon but that the moon does rotate around on its axis, just as Earth does. Carry the ball around the students in a counterclockwise direction to show how the moon would look if it did not rotate on its axis. Point the sticky note toward the front of the room. Now, demonstrate how this looks as the moon rotates while orbiting Earth. Point out that the sticky note on the moon always faces the students (Earth). Be sure they see that the mark is pointing in different directions as it moves around Earth, since the moon gradually rotates on its axis. It takes about the same length of time for the moon to rotate once as it takes to go around Earth once. Follow up with a review of the Moon's phases by using the information below and the transparency of page 15.

Phases of the Moon

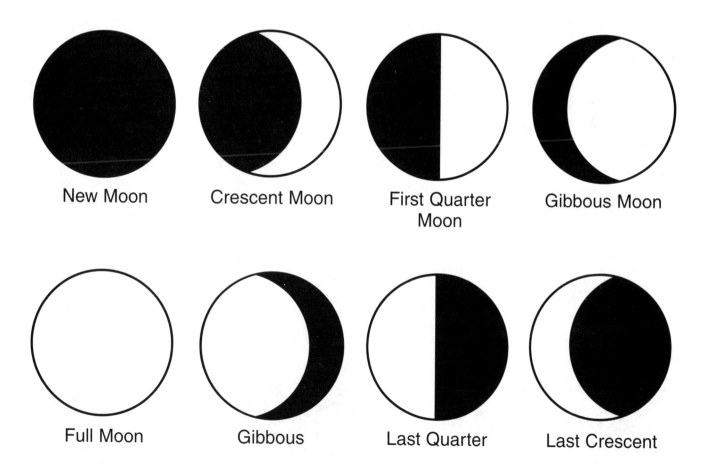

New Moon   Crescent Moon   First Quarter Moon   Gibbous Moon

Full Moon   Gibbous   Last Quarter   Last Crescent

Moon Shapes *(cont.)*

Moon Phase Cutouts

To the Teacher: Make a transparency of this page and cut out the moon phases.
Optional: Enlarge these cutouts and add adhesive to the back of them to be used on the board.

Moon Shapes *(cont.)*

The Phases of the Moon

Outer Circle: moon positions as viewed from outer space
Inner Circle: moon phases as viewed from Earth

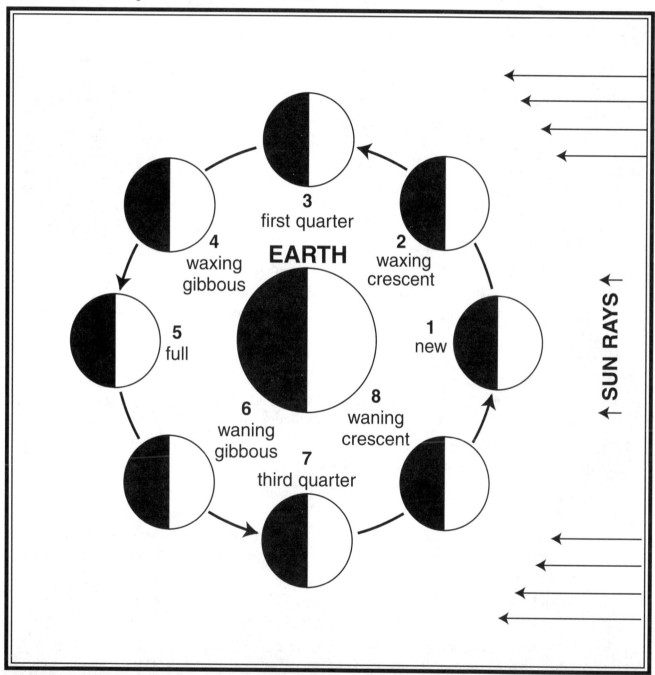

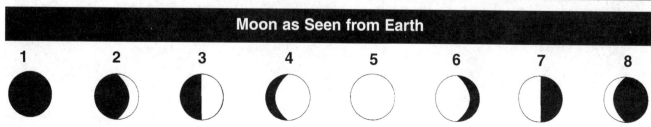

The Moon in Motion

Overview: *Students will make a flipbook of the moon to see how the phases change.*

Materials

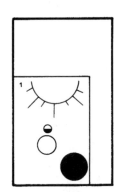

- Moon Flipbook Pages (pages 18 and 19)
- 3" x 5" (8 cm x 13 cm) file cards (16 per flipbook)
- glue
- wide clear packing tape
- rubber bands

Lesson Preparation

- Make enough copies of the flipbook pages for each student. Cut these into sets.
- Make up a set of moon phase pictures and file cards for each student. Glue the #1 picture on the file card of each set as a model for the students. This should be placed in the lower left corner as shown.

Activity

1. Review the moon phases and how they occur. Tell the students that they are going to make a flipbook which will be like a movie of the moon's motion around Earth.

2. Distribute 16 file cards to each student. Show them the model of the first card so they will know where to glue the rest of the pictures on each card.

3. After all pictures have been glued on cards, help students lay these in a pile in numerical order, beginning with card #16.

4. Arrange each set of cards so the lowest edges are slightly offset about ¼ inch (6 mm) above the card underneath. (See drawing on page 17.) This will enable the thumb to flip rapidly through the cards when they are stacked.

5. Hold the card stack in place with a rubber band and flip through them to see if the sun can be seen clearly at the top of the cards and the moons appear to move around Earth.

6. Remove the rubber band and place a long strip of clear packing tape along the back of the cards and overlap the front card for about 1 inch (2.5 cm). This will anchor the cards in place. Run a second strip vertically around the top of the cards. Be sure to avoid locking the cards in place so they will not flip easily. If this happens, use scissors to slide through the tape at the sides until the cards move freely.

The Moon in Motion *(cont.)*

Closure

- Demonstrate to the students how to hold their books at the top in one hand and use their thumbs to flip the pages rapidly, creating the motion-picture effect. Have them do this several times and then discuss the position of sun, moon, and Earth with them as they flip the pages. They should see the moon moving around Earth. Now, have them look only at the moon phases in the lower corner of the cards as they flip the pages. The phases should rapidly change from new through all the phases and return to the new position.

- Relate this motion of the cards to what they have seen in the sky as well as when they used their moon balls in the bright light.

1. Single Card

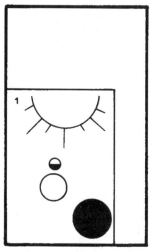

2. Two Cards

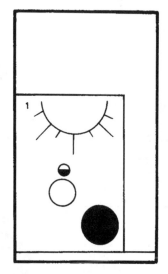

3. Stacked Cards

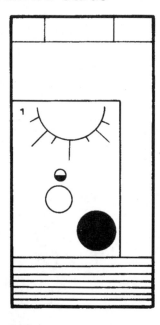

4. Flip book

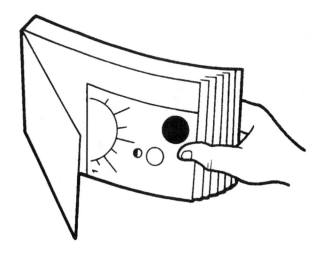

Moon Flipbook Pages

Moon Flipbook Pages (cont.)

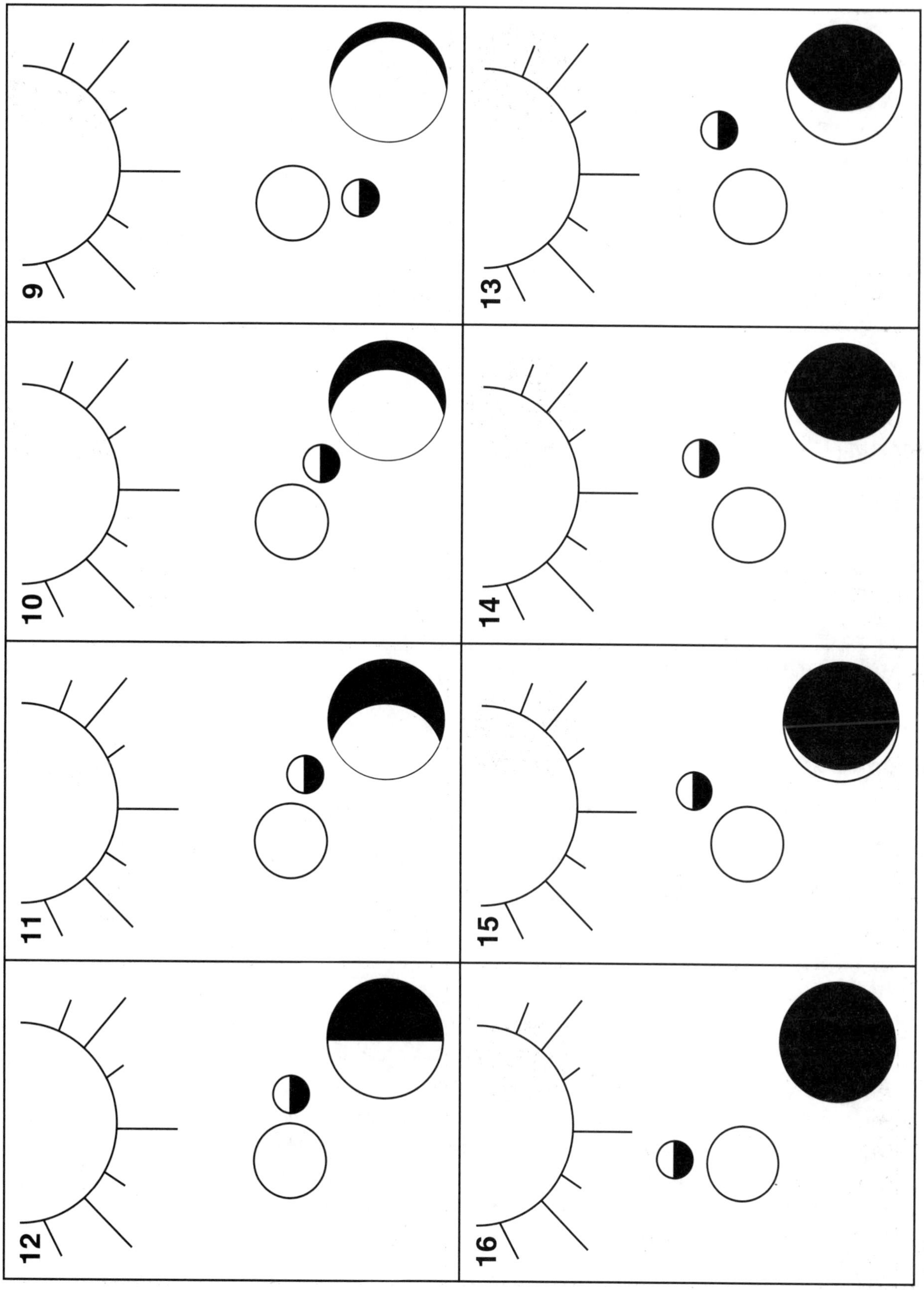

9

10

11

12

13

14

15

16

Star Patterns

The 12 zodiac constellations appear along the path the sun seems to follow in the sky as Earth moves around it. Long ago people thought our lives were controlled by the location of planets in these constellations. Today, we know planets move in orbit around the sun and are seen against a background of zodiac constellations but have no influence on humans. The constellation shapes form a useful map of the sky which helps locate planets, comets, and other astronomical objects. A planet looks like an extra star in a constellation but gradually appears to move into the next constellation as it orbits around the sun.

The next activities will familiarize students with some constellations they will enjoy looking for. Plan these lessons for winter months when the sky is dark early and many of the brightest and largest constellations (e.g., Orion) are visible.

Overview: *Students will learn about the zodiac constellations.*

Materials

- transparencies of Zodiac Constellations (pages 22–24)
- large black construction paper
- copies of The Big Bear (page 34)
- Styrofoam ball (used in moon activity)
- globe or ball to represent Earth
- basketball
- white crayon

Lesson Preparation

- Make transparencies of the Zodiac Constellations. Project each constellation onto a piece of large black construction paper, enlarged to fill the paper. Trace each constellation with white crayon, connecting stars as shown. Write the number on the constellation charts to keep them in order.
- Enlarge copies of the picture of each constellation (e.g., bull for Taurus) and glue these in one corner of the paper.

Activity

1. Ask students if they have seen any star patterns in the sky. Tell them these patterns are called *constellations*. On the board, have students draw constellations with which they may be familiar. Tell them they are going to begin studying constellations.

2. Select 12 students and distribute the constellation pictures to them. Take the class outside to a large field. Bring the basketball, Styrofoam ball, and globe. Have students with the pictures stand in a large circle. The numbers of the pictures will be in order from right to left, as they appear in the sky as Earth moves in a counterclockwise direction around the sun.

Star Patterns *(cont.)*

Activity *(cont.)*

3. Select a student to hold the globe and another to hold the moon ball. Place them in the center of the circle. Have the rest of the students stand within the circle.

4. Give the basketball to one student. Tell the children that this ball will represent the sun. Have the sun stand between the children and the circle of constellations.

5. Explain that although we cannot feel any motion, Earth is moving. Remind students of what they learned about Earth's motion in the lesson Me and My Shadow—that Earth spins on its axis every 24 hours, giving us day and night.

   Have the child who is holding the globe begin to spin it counterclockwise on its axis to demonstrate Earth's motion. Tell the students that at the same time, the moon is slowly moving around Earth. Remind the students of their study of moon phases and point out that from Earth a viewer would see the moon changing phases.

6. Have the child holding the globe begin to walk around the sun in a counterclockwise path; the moon should continue to slowly circle the earth. Point out that from Earth, it appears as if the sun is moving across the sky, gradually moving toward the east.

7. Explain that the stars are very far from Earth, farther than the moon and sun as well as all the other planets. Show the order of the constellations and explain that these star patterns were noticed long ago by people who studied the sky. They discovered that it looked as if the sun traveled in front of these constellations, returning to about the same position a year later.

8. Have the students acting as Earth and the moon stop moving. Remove the moon so students can concentrate on Earth and the sun. Show that from Earth you would not see the constellation which was behind the sun because it is too bright. The constellations you would see would be in the opposite direction. Point to the constellations which would be visible if Earth were in the position it is in this model. Let Earth continue to follow its orbit around the sun and then stop again. Have students pick the constellations which could *not* be seen at this time. Let them tell which constellations would be visible (*those opposite the sun and Earth*).

9. Have other students try the Earth/sun walk to see how the constellations change.

Closure

Poke holes where the stars appear on the black constellation charts. Make the holes different sizes, depending upon the size of the dot for the star. Tape these pictures to the window in order, running right to left. The stars will be made visible as the sunlight shines through the holes in the chart. This will help students become familiar with the constellation shapes and thus find them easier to locate in the night sky.

Star Patterns *(cont.)*

Zodiac Constellations

To the Teacher: On each picture below, the month stating when the constellation is visible is the best month to see it. However, it will also be visible the month before and after. Visibility of these constellations also depends on your latitude.

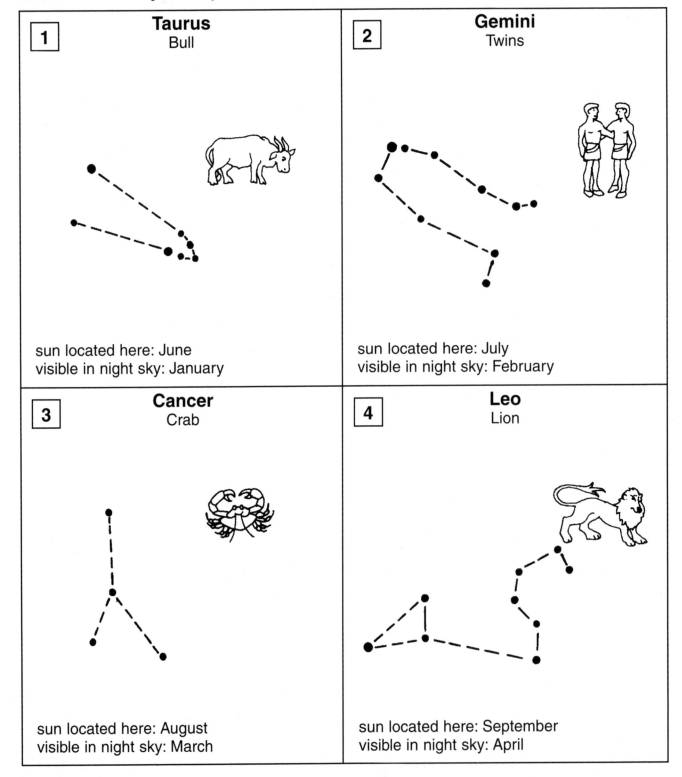

1 **Taurus**
Bull

sun located here: June
visible in night sky: January

2 **Gemini**
Twins

sun located here: July
visible in night sky: February

3 **Cancer**
Crab

sun located here: August
visible in night sky: March

4 **Leo**
Lion

sun located here: September
visible in night sky: April

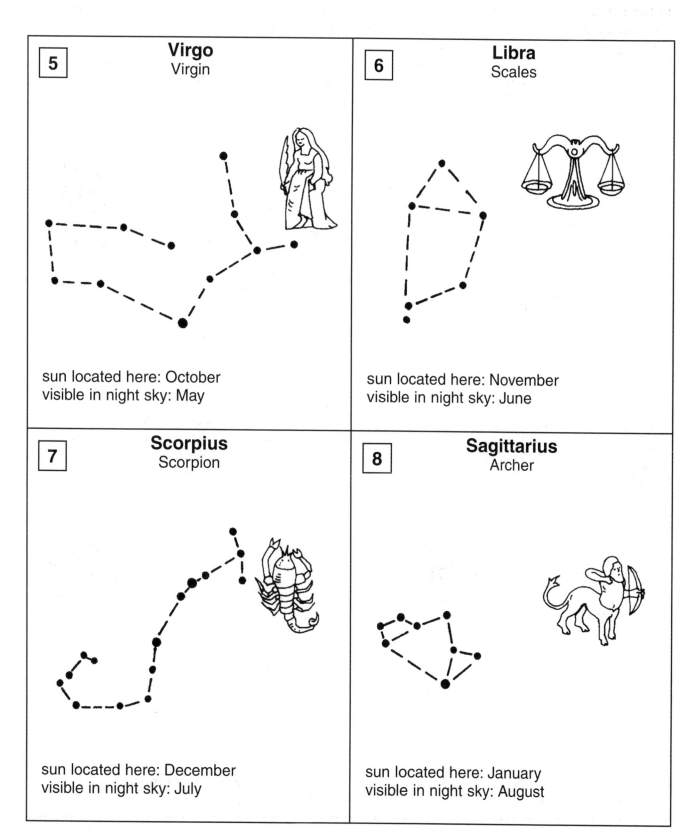

5 **Virgo**
Virgin

sun located here: October
visible in night sky: May

6 **Libra**
Scales

sun located here: November
visible in night sky: June

7 **Scorpius**
Scorpion

sun located here: December
visible in night sky: July

8 **Sagittarius**
Archer

sun located here: January
visible in night sky: August

Zodiac Constellations (cont.)

---

9 Capricornus
Goat

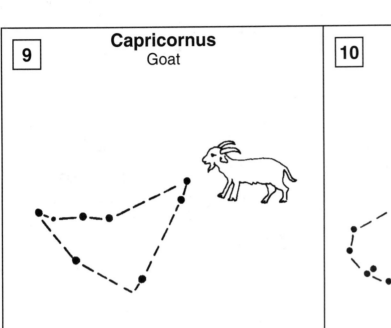

sun located here: February
visible in night sky: September

---

10 Aquarius
Water Bearer

sun located here: March
visible in night sky: October

---

11 Pisces
Fish (2)

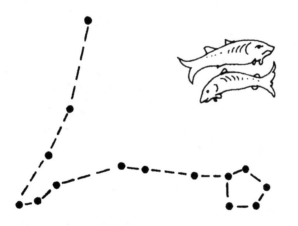

sun located here: April
visible in night sky: November

---

12 Aries
Ram

sun located here: May
visible in night sky: December

Pictures in the Sky

Overview: *Students will become familiar with constellations visible at the current season.*

Materials: transparency and copies of seasonal constellation charts on pages 27–30 and zodiac constellations found on pages 22–24, scissors, black butcher paper and white crayons, glue, file folders, copies of parent letter (page 26)

Lesson Preparation

- Cover a bulletin board with black butcher paper. Make a transparency of the seasonal constellation chart for the current season. Project it onto black paper and use white crayon to trace the stars and connecting lines for the constellations. Outline the Milky Way as it spreads among the stars. Trace the dotted line which is the *ecliptic*—the path the sun and planets appear to follow across the sky.
- Copy the zodiac constellations for this season; they should match those on the seasonal constellation chart. Cut them out, glue them on one page, and white out lines connecting stars. Make a transparency and student copies of these zodiac constellations.
  Note: Some zodiac constellations formed by very faint stars are not shown on these charts. For this activity, include copies of these missing constellations which are visible for this season.
- Make a copy of the current constellation chart for each student. Mount them inside a file folder to make them sturdy.

Activity

1. Review zodiac constellations with the transparencies. Explain that long ago people looked into the sky and saw a way to connect stars to form pictures of animals, people, and familiar objects. Show students constellations visible in the current night sky and drawings of the pictures made by connecting these stars. Ask them if the stars look like their pictures (*many do not*).
2. Distribute copies of the zodiac constellations for this season without the connecting lines. Tell students that they should look at the stars and connect them to make their own pictures of animals or objects. Use one of the constellations on the transparency as an example and have students suggest a new picture. Draw lines on the transparency to create the new picture. Tell them to give their constellation a name.
3. Have students share their new constellations in groups.
4. Show students the seasonal constellation chart on the black paper to see what tonight's sky will look like. Point out the Milky Way and ask if they have ever seen this. Say that it looks like a hazy river across the sky, very faint so it can only be seen away from city lights. Tell them that long ago people believed it looked like spilled milk, thus the name.

Closure

Distribute copies of the current constellation chart and parent letter to students. Explain that they are to match the chart with the stars in the sky every night for the next week. Tell them it is important that the sky be dark and without too many clouds. Say the class will discuss what they observe at the next meeting.

Pictures in the Sky *(cont.)*

Parent Letter for Sky Observations

To the Teacher: Distribute this letter with the seasonal constellation chart.

Date_____

Dear Parents,

Now that we have observed the moon and learned about its phases, we are turning our attention to the stars. Your child has received a constellation chart for the current season. The students have done a variety of activities to help them recognize the shapes of some of the most prominent constellations that can be seen at this time of the year. It is now time to try to match these pictures with the stars they see in the real sky.

If it is clear tonight, please go outside with your child to help him or her find these star patterns. You will need to go where it is dark, away from house and street lights if possible. It will be helpful to have a dim flashlight to look at the chart while matching it to the stars. If the flashlight is too bright, cover it with your fingers and let only a little light filter through. This will help your eyes stay adjusted to the dark.

When using the chart, face south and hold the chart with north at the top. Try to locate one of the brightest constellations first. The larger the dot (star) on the chart, the brighter the star will appear.

Each day, we will be discussing what the children were able to see in the sky during the previous night.

Thank you for helping your child learn about the constellations. The other three seasonal constellations charts will be distributed to the students at the end of our study. This will enable the children and their families to continue their study of the sky throughout the year.

Cordially,

_____

Pictures in the Sky (cont.)

Fall Constellations

The gray patch represents the Milky Way, an area of faint light coming from the distant stars at the outer edge of the galaxy in which we live (Milky Way Galaxy). This area reminded ancient astronomers of spilled milk, so they named it the *Milky Way*.

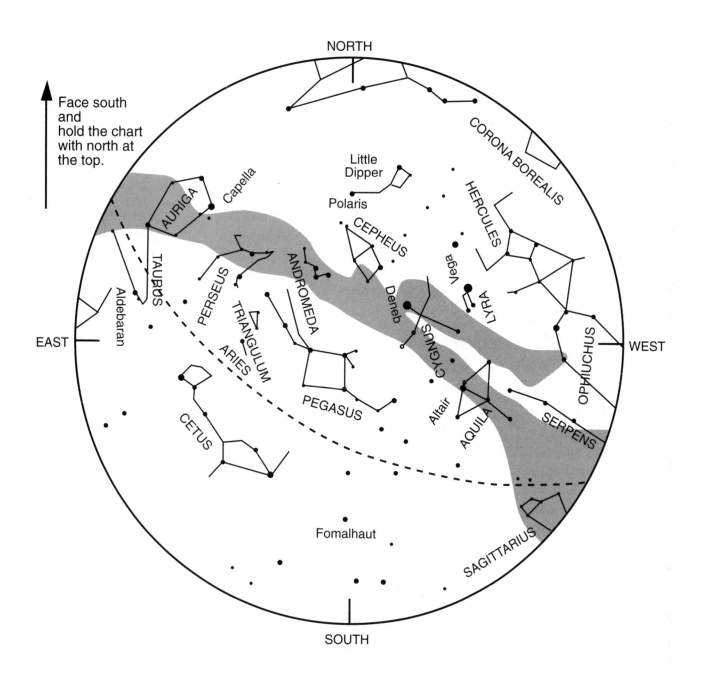

Pictures in the Sky *(cont.)*

Winter Constellations

The gray patch represents the Milky Way, an area of faint light coming from the distant stars at the outer edge of the galaxy in which we live (Milky Way Galaxy). This area reminded ancient astronomers of spilled milk, so they named it the *Milky Way*.

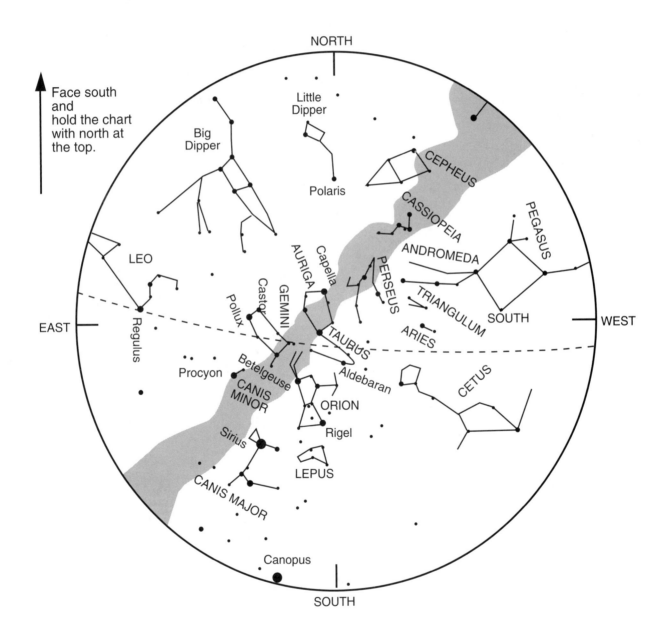

Pictures in the Sky *(cont.)*

Spring Constellations

The gray patch represents the Milky Way, an area of faint light coming from the distant stars at the outer edge of the galaxy in which we live (Milky Way Galaxy). This area reminded ancient astronomers of spilled milk, so they named it the *Milky Way*.

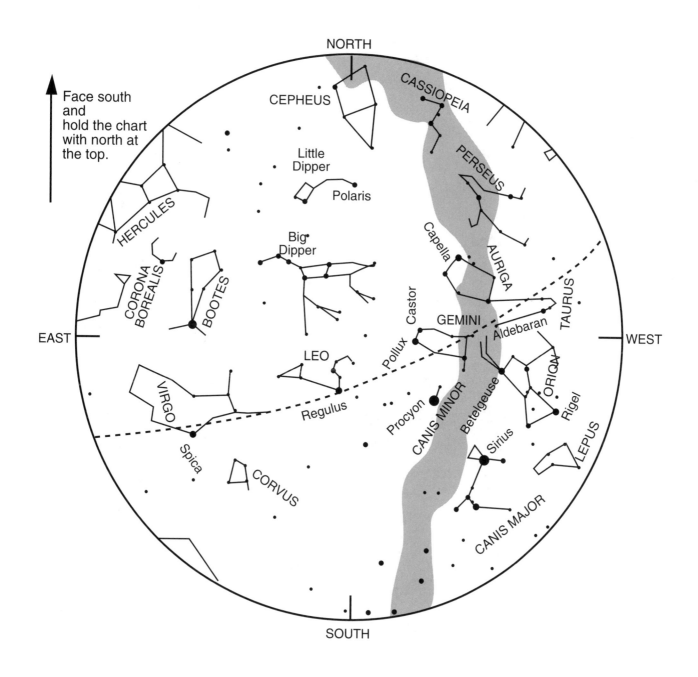

Pictures in the Sky *(cont.)*

Summer Constellations

The gray patch represents the Milky Way, an area of faint light coming from the distant stars at the outer edge of the galaxy in which we live (Milky Way Galaxy). This area reminded ancient astronomers of spilled milk, so they named it the *Milky Way*.

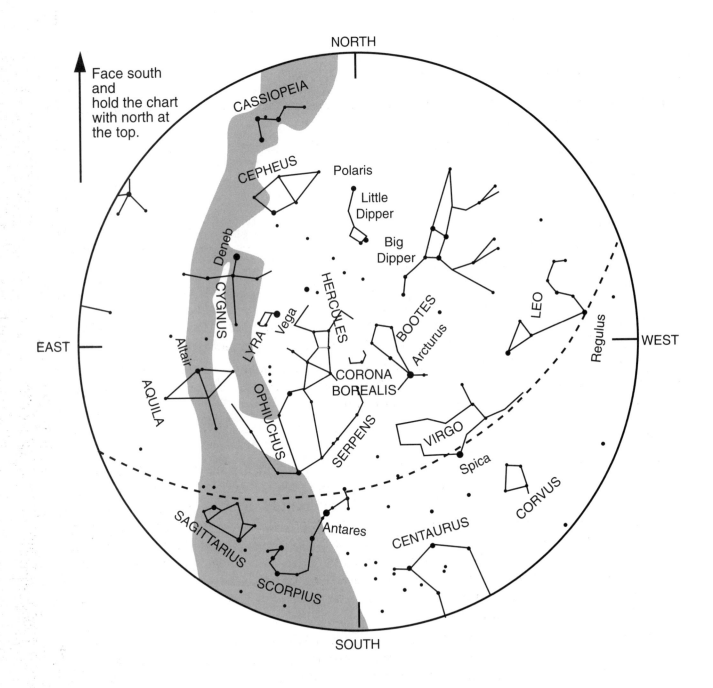

The Big Bear

Overview: *Students will see how stars are used to form constellations.*

Materials

- seasonal constellations and North Polar Constellations charts on black paper.
- transparency and copies of pages 33 and 34
- scissors
- crayons
- glue
- transparency and copies of page 32
- black butcher paper

Lesson Preparation

- Use the transparency of the North Polar Constellations and white crayon to make a large copy on the black butcher paper.
- Connect the dots on the transparency of the activity sheet and superimpose it on the drawing of the bear on page 34.

Activity

1. Review constellations students have seen during their past viewing sessions. Point out the new chart showing North Polar Constellations. Explain that these constellations are so high in the sky that they can be seen during most of the year.

2. Point out the Big Dipper on the chart. Tell students this is an easy constellation to find. Show how the pointer stars show the way to Polaris, the star over Earth's North Pole. Polaris does not move in the sky like all the other stars which rotate clockwise around it as Earth spins on its axis. For travelers, Polaris became the most important star to follow and not get lost.

3. Distribute a copy of The Dipper in the Bear activity to each student. Explain that they are to connect the numbered dots with pencil and the letters with crayon. When finished, they can cut out this picture and glue it inside the picture of the bear.

Closure

- Show a transparency of the Dipper inside Ursa Major and point out the shape of the dipper. Tell students that some cultures saw this group of stars as a plow, a dipper, or a long-handled pot. The Indians thought this group and other stars in this area looked like a big and little bear with long tails. They knew that bears did not have long tails, so they made up a story to explain it. An Indian brave was being chased by a mother bear and her cub. He became tired of running and decided to stop and fight. He grabbed both bears by their short tails and began to swing them around his head. Their tails began to stretch longer and longer. Finally, he let go and the bears flew up into the sky and turned into stars. There they remain to this day, swinging around the star Polaris at the tip of the little bear's tail.

- Arrange a family observing night at the school so all can look at the constellations and moon. Plan this on a night when the moon is between four and eight days old so that it will not be so bright the stars cannot be seen. Arrange to bring a telescope or binoculars to look at the moon.

The Big Bear *(cont.)*

The North Polar Constellations

Instructions: Face north and rotate the chart so the present month is at the top. This should match your view at about 9 P.M. If you are using this before 9 P.M., rotate the chart slightly counterclockwise.

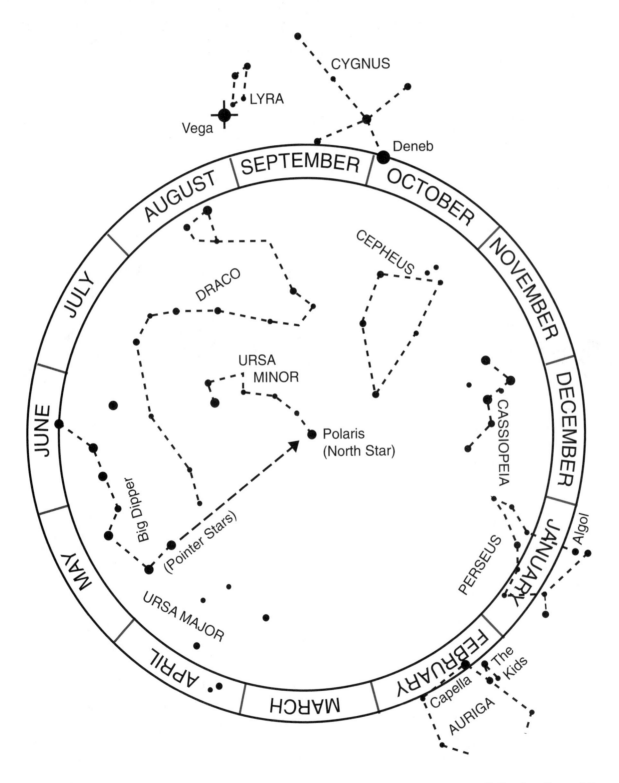

The Big Bear *(cont.)*

The Dipper in the Bear

To the Student: Connect the dots to find a picture of a dipper and a bear.

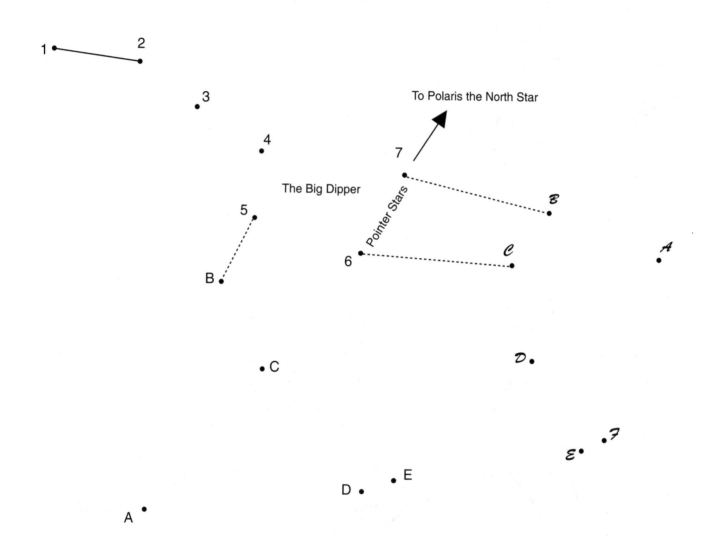

The Big Bear (cont.)

Ursa Major

34

More About the Dipper

Overview: *Students will learn how to use the Dipper to find other constellations and tell time by it. They will also make a model of it and see what it will look like in the future.*

Materials

- transparency and copies of pages 37 and 39
- copies of page 38
- transparency of page 29
- black spray paint
- string or thick thread
- copy of page 40 for each student

- shoeboxes with lids for every 5 students
- aluminum foil
- scissors
- clear tape
- brass fasteners, one per student

Lesson Preparation

Paint the shoeboxes black inside, including the lid. Cut off one of the short ends of the box so that it will be a window through which to view the hanging stars.

Enlarge the image of the Big Dipper Today, shown in Changes in the Dipper (page 39), so it will fit at one end of the shoebox. Make enough copies for each group to use.

Activities

1. Show the transparency of the Spring Constellations and point out the constellations Big and Little Dippers, Leo, Virgo, and Bootes. Show the transparency of The Big Dipper's Magic Arrows (page 37), and distribute a copy of it to each student. Tell them to follow the instructions to find how to use the Dipper to locate these constellations. Explain that they should fill in the blanks on this page. The answers are: (1) Little Dipper, (2) Leo, (3) kite shaped, and (4) Virgo

2. Divide the students into groups of four or five and distribute a copy of Making a Model of the Big Dipper (page 38) to each of them. Explain that although we see these stars in the pattern of a dipper from Earth, they are not all the same distance from us. Astronomers measure distances in space in light years, the distance light can travel in a year. Light travels at 186,322 miles (310,536 km) per second, so a light year is about 6 trillion miles (10,000,000,000,000 km).

3. Distribute a shoebox and lid, thread, aluminum foil, scissors, clear tape, and enlarged image of the Big Dipper Today.

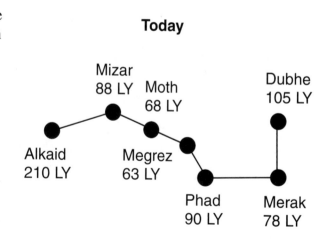

Today

Mizar 88 LY Moth 68 LY Dubhe 105 LY

Alkaid 210 LY Megrez 63 LY

Phad 90 LY Merak 78 LY

More About the Dipper *(cont.)*

Activities *(cont.)*

3. Show the transparency of Changes in the Dipper and describe how the star patterns the students hung in their shoeboxes change. Explain how the Dipper has changed and will continue to do so in the future. Point out how the stars Alkaid and Dubhe moved during the 100,000 years. Tell students that all the constellations we see will change their shapes in the future because the stars gradually move at different speeds and in different directions.

4. Distribute a copy of the Star Clock (page 40), scissors, and a brass brad to each student. Read and discuss the information and then, cut out the two parts of the clock. Assist them as necessary to assemble the clock.

50,000 Years Ago

Today

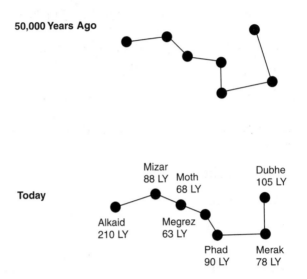

50,000 Years from Now

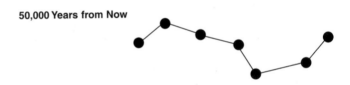

Closure

- Send the Star Clock home with the students, along with a note they write to their parents, explaining how to use it. You may need to let them do this assignment over a few days if the night sky is overcast.

- Have the students write a letter to their parents telling them what they have learned thus far about constellations and stars. Encourage them to include drawings.

Extender

- Remove the letters, lines and arrows from The Dipper in the Bear (page 33) so that only the dots for the stars appear. Distribute a copy of this to each student. Have students draw new constellations from these stars.

- Have the students coordinate a way of sharing what they have learned with another class.

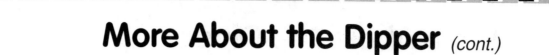

More About the Dipper (cont.)

The Big Dipper's Magic Arrows

To the Student: Use the Big Dipper to help find other nearby stars and constellations. The names of constellations on this chart are all written in CAPITAL letters.

Instructions

1. Use the pointer stars at the end of the bowl of the Big Dipper to locate the North Star, Polaris. What is the constellation to which Polaris is attached? _____

2. Return to the Big Dipper and pretend to fill the bowl with water. Poke an imaginary hole in the bowl. The water will now drip across the sky and fall on the back of a lion named _____.

3. Trace the arc in the handle of the dipper and "arc to Arcturus." This is a giant red star at the base of Boötes, which is shaped like a _____. This star is much larger than our sun. If it were in the center of our solar system, it would stretch all the way out to the orbit of Mars!

4. Now, slide across the sky from Arcturus to Spica, a bright star in the constellation _____.

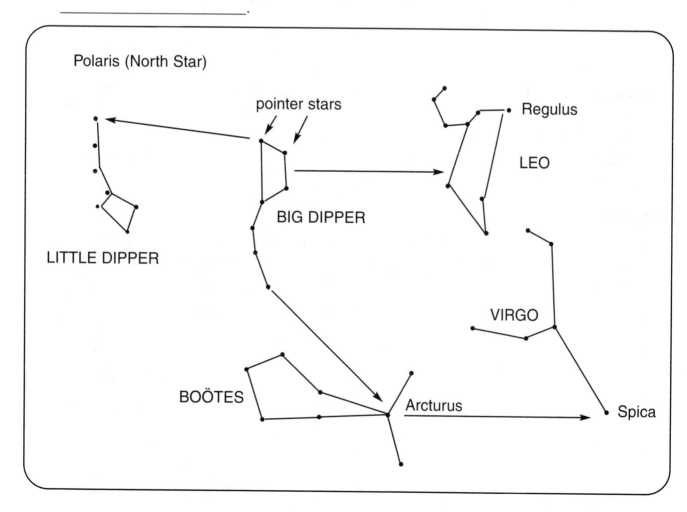

Making a Model of the Big Dipper

Materials: shoebox, lid (sprayed black inside), black thread, aluminum foil, scissors, clear tape, picture of the Big Dipper as seen today (page 39)

Instructions

1. Cut seven pieces of thread about 6 inches (18 cm) long. Tape them to the dots on this template so that they will hang straight down from the dots.

2. Make seven small balls from the foil and tie each to the end of the string so it is level with the X. Cut away the extra string.

3. Trim this template so it will fit inside the shoebox lid and then tape it in place so the E will be at the cutaway end.

4. Glue the Big Dipper picture inside the shoebox opposite the opening.

5. Put the box on a table and look directly into it from about eight inches (20 cm) away. As you look from Earth, you see the pattern of a dipper, even though the stars are not all the same distance. Compare what you see with the picture of the Big Dipper at the back of the box.

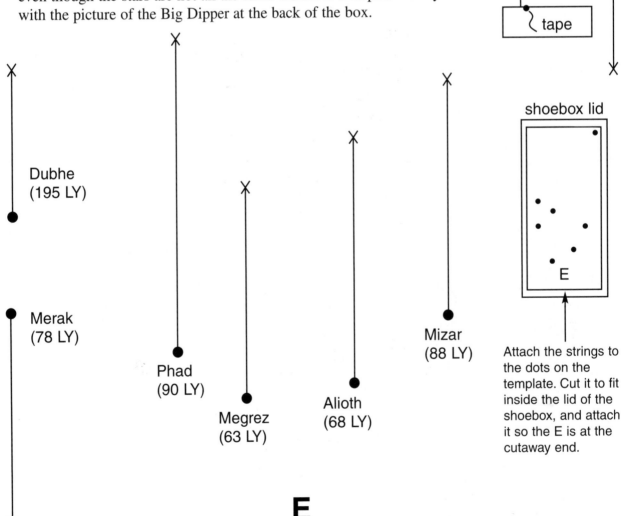

Alkaid
(210 LY)

tape

Dubhe
(195 LY)

Merak
(78 LY)

Phad
(90 LY)

Megrez
(63 LY)

Alioth
(68 LY)

Mizar
(88 LY)

shoebox lid

Attach the strings to the dots on the template. Cut it to fit inside the lid of the shoebox, and attach it so the E is at the cutaway end.

E

More About the Dipper *(cont.)*

Changes in the Dipper

The stars that form the Big Dipper are slowly moving, and thus the shape of this constellation looked different in the past and will continue to change.

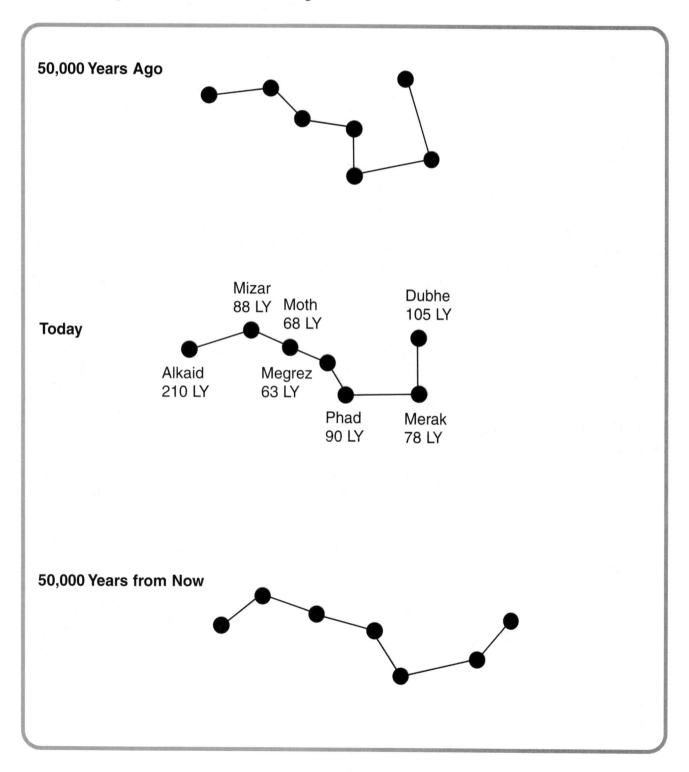

50,000 Years Ago

Mizar
88 LY

Moth
68 LY

Dubhe
105 LY

Today

Alkaid
210 LY

Megrez
63 LY

Phad
90 LY

Merak
78 LY

50,000 Years from Now

More About the Dipper *(cont.)*

Star Clock

To the Student: Although our earth does not seem to be moving, it is really spinning fast. If you watch the stars, they look like they move around Earth. Long ago, people thought they did. Today, we know Earth is spinning on its axis, making the stars appear to move around us.

The circumference of the Earth at the equator is about 24,000 miles (40,000 km). Earth spins once in 24 hours. Circle how fast you would be spinning in miles (km) per hour at the equator.

2,400 (4,000 km)   1,000 (600 km)   24 (40 km)

You spin slower as you move from the equator to the poles, where you would be standing still. The north end of Earth's axis points to Polaris, the North Star. All the other stars seem to be making circles around Polaris. See how the Big Dipper can be used as a clock as it circles the North Star.

Directions: Cut out and assemble the Star Clock circles so the smaller circle (Time) is over the larger one. Line up the two black dots and poke a hole through them. Push a brass fastener through these to hold the two circles together.

Take a Star Clock out at night and look for the Big and Little Dippers. Turn the clock until the present month is at the top. Turn the Big Dipper around until it matches up with what you see in the sky. Look at the time through the window. It should show the approximate real time.

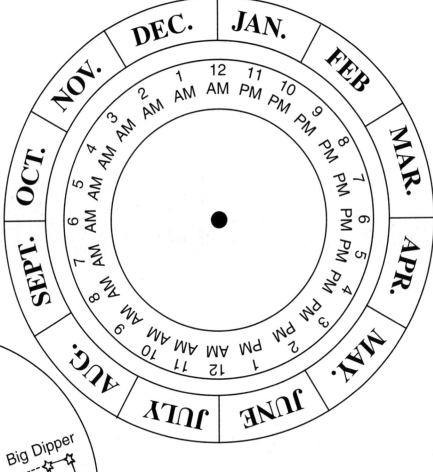

Scale Model of the Planets

Overview: *Students will learn the sizes of the planets and compare them to Earth.*

Materials

- one piece each of red, gray, blue, white, and black construction paper approximately 6" (15 cm) square
- piece of white and yellow 4' x 1' (120 cm x 30 cm) butcher paper
- piece of blue and orange 2' x 1' (60 cm x 30 cm) butcher paper
- meter stick
- 15 yards (13.5 m) string
- four index cards
- compass to draw circles
- pencil
- tape

Lesson Preparation

- Make paper scale models of the five smallest planets by drawing a circle according to the radius sizes and colors of paper indicated on the chart below.

Planet	Paper Color	Circle Radius
Mercury	gray	1.9 cm
Venus	white	4.8 cm
Earth	blue	5.0 cm
Mars	red	2.7 cm
Pluto (dwarf planet)	black	0.9 cm

Scale: Earth's radius of 3,837 miles (6,378 km) = 5 cm

Scale Model of the Planets *(cont.)*

Lesson Preparation *(cont.)*

- Using the same scale, make larger circles or half circles to show the four largest planets. Since the compass is not large enough to draw circles of these planets, cut strings which are the lengths of the radius, leaving extra string at each end so one end can be tied to an index card and the other can be tied into a loop. Put the name of the planet on the card with its string attached. Place the paper on the floor and have someone hold the card in the center of the paper while you put the pencil in the loop at the other end, stretch the string taut, and draw the circle. For the larger planets, hold the card in the center of the long edge of the paper and then stretch the string with the pencil to draw a half circle.

Planet	Paper Color	Circle Radius
Jupiter	white	56 cm
Saturn	yellow	47 cm
Uranus	green	20 cm
Neptune	blue	19.5 cm

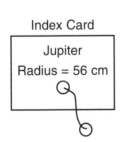
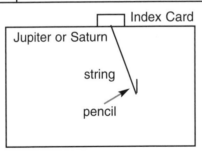
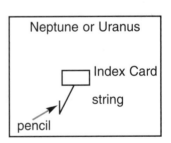

- Cut string to represent the sun's diameter—about 870,000 miles (1,392,000 km). Using the same scale as used for planets, the string will be 10.9 meters, 109 times the diameter of Earth.

Activity

1. Place planet models on the board (or floor) in order from largest to smallest. Show students the Earth model and label it. Say that the diameter of our planet is 7,973 miles (12,756 km) but that the circle is only 10 cm across. Explain that other planets have been reduced to show how big they are compared to Earth.

2. Let students pick which planets they think are Jupiter, Mars, and Pluto (dwarf planet). Do not correct them if they are wrong.

Scale Model of the Planets (cont.)

Activity (cont.)

3. Label all planets. Begin with Jupiter and place on the board as in the diagram below. Tape in place, except for Earth.

(1) Earth

(2) Venus

(3) Mars

(4) Mercury

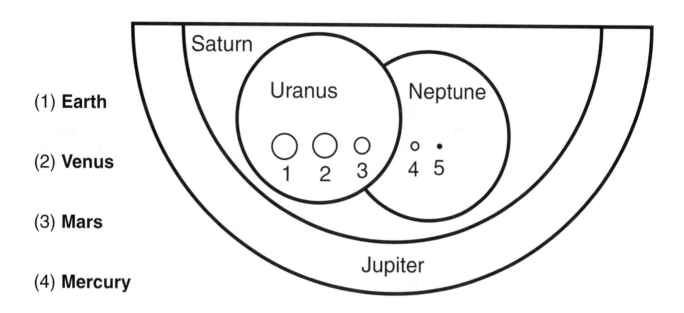

(5) Pluto (dwarf planet)

4. Fold the Earth model in half and let students estimate how many "Earths" would fit across the diameter of Jupiter. Write the extremes of their estimates on the board.

5. Begin measuring how many Earths will fit across the diameter, using the Earth circle placed at one end of the diameter and moving it along. Have students help count, stopping halfway to ask them to make another estimate. Update the estimates on the board. Continue counting the remaining number of Earths (about 11) that fit across Jupiter.

6. Compare the smaller planets to Earth. Point out that Venus is nearly the same size as Earth and Mars is about half that.

7. Show students that Uranus and Neptune are nearly the same size. Fold one in half to compare the diameters with that of Jupiter, using the same technique as used with Earth's model.

Closure

- Take students outside to compare the string which represents the sun's diameter with the planets. Have two students hold the models of the planets and begin stretching the string at one end of Jupiter's diameter, across its length, and then to the end. Be sure students know the sun is a star, not a planet. Explain that stars are different sizes and our sun is an average-size star. Some stars are so huge they would stretch beyond the orbits of Mercury, Venus, and Earth, all the way to Mars.

- Place the scale model of the planets on a bulletin board for the students to look at and become familiar with their sizes.

Scale Model of the Solar System

Overview: *Students will learn the distances between the planets.*

Materials

- at least 300' (100 m) of heavy string
- six pieces of heavy cardboard, approximately 5" x 8" (13 cm x 20 cm)
- three pieces of heavy cardboard, approximately 8" x 10" (20 cm x 26 cm)
- metal washer

Lesson Preparation

- Label small cardboards with the names of the first six planets shown on the chart. Label larger cardboards with the remaining planets. Place a hole in the center of the long edge of each cardboard.
- Tie one end of the string to the card and measure the length of string needed to represent the distance of each planet from the sun as shown on the chart below. Tie a washer to the end of the string to prevent it from fraying. Longer strings are needed for the last four planets. Wind the strings for these planets as you measure them, to avoid their becoming tangled.

Planet	Length of String
Mercury	0.4 meters
Venus	0.7 meters
Earth	1.0 meters
Mars	1.5 meters
Jupiter	5.2 meters
Saturn	9.5 meters
Uranus	19.2 meters
Neptune	30.1 meters
Pluto (dwarf)	39.4 meters

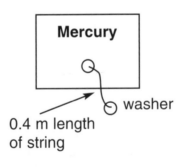

Scale: Earth's average distance of 93 million miles (149 million km) from the sun = one meter

Activity

1. Review the scale model of the planets made in the last lesson. Tell students this lesson will show them the order of the planets from the sun, as well as how far they are away from the sun and each other. Let them know that the scale for this model is very different from the one that was used with the planets. Stretch out the string for Earth and explain that it is only one meter but that our planet is actually 93 million miles (149 million km) from the sun.

2. Select a student to be the sun and stand in the front of the room. Choose four other students, each to take one of the inner planet cards (Mercury through Mars). Have the student with the Mercury string give the end of it to the "sun" and stretch the string across the front of the room. Let each of the remaining three planets follow in the order shown on the chart. Talk about how close these planets are to each other and the sun.

Scale Model of the Solar System *(cont.)*

Activity *(cont.)*

3. Ask another child to stretch out the string for Jupiter. Students will immediately see it is much farther away from the sun than the inner planets. Explain that in the space between Mars and Jupiter there are many small planets called *asteroids*. Scientists think these formed at the same time as all the other planets but never pulled together to form one planet.

4. Explain that in order to show the rest of the solar system, they will need to move outside. Have the string for the five planets wound on their cardboards.

5. Take students to a field outside which is at least 40 meters long. Select three students to be the sun and have them stand side by side, facing the end of the field.

6. Give the planet cards to nine students. Have them stretch out the four inner planets' strings, letting one "sun" hold the washers at the ends of the strings. The strings will be stretched in one line. Let the students stretch out the planets in order, waiting until one string is fully extended before beginning the next. Divide the strings among the remaining two "suns." Have students lay the strings on the ground and return to the sun's position.

7. Explain that all planets move in the same direction around the sun but not at the same speed. The closer the planet is to the sun, the faster it moves. Mercury takes only 88 days to go once around the sun. Earth takes 365 days for this trip. Pluto (a dwarf planet) is the slowest, taking 248 years to get around the sun once. This means the planets do not travel around the sun in a straight line, as the strings are now laid out.

Closure

- Take a "walk" along the solar system, pointing out that the inner four planets are small, rocky, and very close together. Point out that Jupiter through Neptune are huge, mostly made of gases, and very far from the sun. Remind students that Pluto is a dwarf planet and, like the inner planets, it is rocky.

- Have one student return to the sun's position and let students see how small he or she appears from the distance of Pluto. Explain that if they were on Pluto, the sun would be only a small star in the distance. Since the sun is so far away, the sky would always be dark, and the stars could be seen all the time.

- As students walk back to the sun, tell them the farther we get from the sun, the colder it gets. So planets beyond Mars are very cold. When you reach Mars, explain that its temperature is cold but it has been thought that people might someday live there. They will need special space suits to keep warm and to stay at the same air pressure as that of Earth. If this is so, they will also need tanks of air to breathe, just as astronauts did when they went to the moon.

- As you pass Earth, explain that it is getting very hot as they get nearer the sun. It would not be possible for people to live on Venus because of its poisonous atmosphere and great heat. When you reach Mercury, let them know that it would be so hot there that the metal lead would melt.

- Read *The Magic School Bus® Lost in the Solar System*. (See page 48.)

Making a Comet

Teacher Information

Scientists believe that comets formed at the same time as our solar system, about 4.6 billion years ago. They orbit the sun, some return regularly while others appear only once. The famous Comet Halley, last seen in 1985-86, returns every 76 years and was named for the astronomer who was the first to calculate its orbit and predict when it would return. The nucleus of the Comet Halley is about 3 miles (5 km) in diameter yet its tail, in 1910, stretched for 150 million miles (240 million kilometers) as it passed by the sun. It consists of gases such as hydrogen, oxygen, methane, ammonia, sodium, and hydrogen, in a frozen state until vaporized as the comet nears the sun. The rest of the core is composed of solid substances, probably dust and stony materials much like fine sand.

Overview: Ingredients of a comet will be mixed by the teacher to simulate the real thing.

Materials

- 10 pounds (4.5 kg) dry ice
- large plastic bag
- gloves
- 2 spoonfuls of sand
- tray or large bowl
- hammer
- transparency of Parts of a Comet
- pinch of salt

Demonstration

1. Wrap the dry ice in newspaper and use the hammer to break it into small pieces about the size of tennis balls. Be careful to wear gloves while doing this. (Do not allow students to handle the dry ice.) Put the pieces into the plastic bag and then, fold it open on the tray or in the bowl.

2. Add the following ingredients to the dry ice and compare them to comet material as you do so. Have the students listen to the hissing sound made as the water begins to thaw the dry ice. The comet would sound just like this if they were standing on it. Pieces would also be bursting off as jets of gases escape and blow away pieces of the comet.

Comet Recipe	
Ingredient	**Comet Material**
2 cups water	hydrogen and oxygen
3-4 drops ammonia	ammonia gas
2-3 spoonfuls sand	solid material in nucleus
pinch of salt	sodium

Closure

Tell the students that the vapor coming off the dry ice is the coma. Blow on the comet, like the solar wind, to send the vapor away from you, creating the long tail of the comet. Give the comet a name and let it sit out where students can see it evaporate throughout the day.

Making a Comet (cont.)

Parts of a Comet

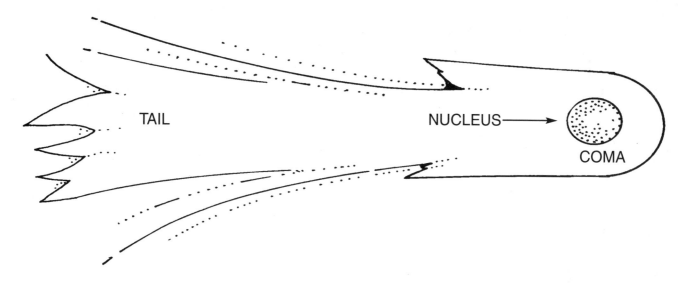

Nucleus: The nucleus is the center of the comet. It is made of frozen gas, dust and rock. It is usually one to 10 miles (16 km) across.

Coma: The coma is a fuzzy glowing ball made from the evaporating frozen gases in the nucleus as the comet gets near the sun's heat. It can be as large as 100,000 miles (166,667 km) across, or about half the distance from the Earth to the moon. The largest coma ever recorded by astronomers was even larger than the sun, which is 870,000 miles (1,450,000 km) in diameter.

Tail: Comets may have two tails, one made of gases and the other of dust. The tail of the comet is created by the solar winds blasting against the coma, forcing the evaporating gases away from the sun. The tail always points away from the sun, even when the comet is moving away and makes it possible to see the comet. It may stretch for millions of miles.

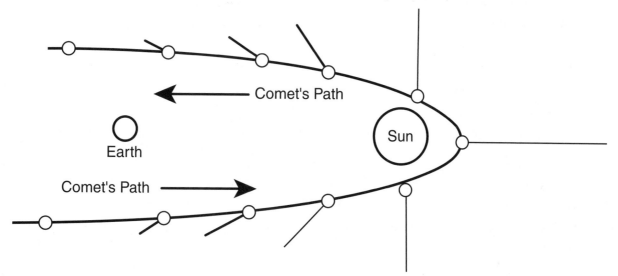

Teacher and Student Resources

Related Books

Cole, Joanna. *The Magic School Bus® Lost in the Solar System.* Scholastic, Inc., 1990. This delightful book takes children on a unique field trip through the solar system aboard the Magic Bus. They travel past each of the nine planets and the asteroid belt.

Van Cleave, Janice. *Astronomy for Every Kid.* John Wiley & Sons, Inc., NY, 1991. Included are activities and projects, with a list of materials, instructions, expected results, and explanations.

Young, Ruth M. *Thematic Unit: Astronomy.* Teacher Created Resources, Inc., 2000. (800) 662-4321. This science/literature unit is filled with activities about planets, moon, sun, comets, and constellations.

Young, Ruth M. *Science/Literature Unit: The Magic School Bus® Lost in the Solar System.* Teacher Created Resources, Inc., 1996. (800) 662-4321. This teacher's guide contains a variety of hands-on activities to teach astronomy concepts, and a script for a simulation flight to the moon.

Suppliers of Science Materials

Abrams Planetarium, Michigan State University, East Lansing, MI 48824
www.pa.msu.edu/abrams/diary.html
Provides a monthly Sky Calendar, with daily astronomical events on one side and the current planets and constellations on the other.

Astronomical Society of the Pacific, (800) 335-2624. (Request a free catalog or order online. Provides books, celestial software, calendars, globes, slide sets, videotapes, DVDs, and posters.)

Delta Education (800) 282-9560. Request a catalog of materials or order online.
http://www.delta-education.com/corp/info/ordernow.html
Supplies a wide variety of materials to support hands-on science in all areas from elementary to middle school.

Dorling Kindersley (DK) http://usstore.dk.com/shop/
Offers books about astronomy online including *The Visual Dictionary of the Universe, The Young Astronomer,* and *Guide to Space: A Photographic Journey Through the Universe.*

Great Explorations in Math and Science (GEMS) Request a catalog or order online.
http://www.lhs.berkeley.edu/GEMS/gemsguides.html
Provides great teacher guides in a wide range of science topics including astronomy such as Moons of Jupiter 1993 by Debra Sutton.

National Geographic (800)447-0647. Request a catalog of materials or order online.
www.nationalgeographic.com/
Supplies maps and posters such as The Heavens, The Earth's Moon, Solar System/Celestial Family and The Universe. Check their Web site for appropriate back issues on astronomy to order.

National Science Teachers Association (NSTA) (800) 277-5300.
http://www.nsta.org/ or the online catalog of materials at http://store.nsta.org/
Provides books, posters, and software related to astronomy and other sciences. Members receive a monthly professional journal, the bimonthly *NSTA Reports.*

Binding

The instructions for each quilt indicate the width to cut the binding used in that project. The measurements are sufficient for a quilt made of flannel fabrics and medium low loft quilt batting. If you use a high loft batt or combine a fluffy high loft batt with flannel fabrics, you may want to increase the width of the binding strips by adding 1/4 to 1/2-inch to the cut width of your binding. Always test a small segment of the binding before cutting all the strips needed.

Step 1 Diagonally piece the binding strips. Fold the strip in half lengthwise, wrong sides together; press.

Stitch diagonally   Trim to 1/4" seam allowance   Press seam open

Double-Layer Binding

Step 2 Unfold and trim one end at a 45° angle. Turn under the edge 1/4-inch; press. Refold the strip.

Fold Line

Step 3 With raw edges of the binding and quilt top even, stitch with a scant 1-inch seam allowance, unless otherwise specified, starting 2-inches from the angled end.

Step 4 Miter the binding at the corners. As you approach a corner of the quilt, stop sewing a scant 1-inch from the corner of the quilt (use the same measurement as your seam allowance). Generally, a 3/8-inch seam allowance is used for regular cotton quilts and often a 1-inch seam allowance is used

for flannel quilts. Each project in this book gives specific instructions for the binding width and seam allowance to be used.

Step 5 Clip the threads and remove the quilt from under the presser foot.

Step 6 Flip the binding strip up and away from the quilt, then fold the binding down even with the raw edge of the quilt. Begin sewing at the upper edge. Miter all 4 corners in this manner.

Step 7 Trim the end of the binding so it can be tucked inside of the beginning binding about 1/2-inch. Finish stitching the seam.

Step 8 Turn the folded edge of the binding over the raw edges and to the back of the quilt so that the stitching line does not show. The corners will naturally turn with very little effort. Pin as needed to create a nice mitered corner on the back as well as on the front. Slip stitch the binding to the backside of the quilt by hand. To do this, slip your needle into the quilt back, sliding the needle approximately 1/4-inch. Bring it out of the fabric again and catch a few threads in the fold of the binding. At exactly the same point from which the needle emerged, insert it into the quilt back again, and take the next stitch. It is a good idea to take a double stitch approximately every 6 to 8-inches to anchor the binding.

Thank you to the Staff of Thimbleberries® Design Studio;

Sue Bahr, Lisa Kirchoff, Kathy Lobeck, Ardelle Paulson,
Sherry Husske, Virginia Brodd, Renae Ashwill, Julie Jergens,
Tracy Schrantz, Clarine Howe, Pearl Baysinger,
Ellen Carter, and quilters Julie Borg and Leone Rusch.

Publishing
P
S
Solutions